FORTY GOATS

A BALLAD

Discreetly dedicated to I. B. and W. H.

DAVID Z CROOKES

All rights reserved. No part of this publication may be reproduced, stored in a retrieval system or transmitted, in any form or by any means, electronic, mechanical, photocopying, recording or otherwise, without the prior permission of the author.

Printed in 2022 by Shanway Press,
15 Crumlin Road, Belfast BT14 6AA

ISBN: 978-1-910044-43-8

© 2022 David Z Crookes

A STRANGE KIND OF FOREWORD

The Cattle Raid of Cooley

Bendacht ar cech óen mebraigfes go
hindraic taín amlaidseo &
na tuillfe cruth aile furri.

Sed ego qui scripsi hanc historiam aut
uerius fabulam, quibusdam fidem in hac
historia aut fabula non accommodo.
Quaedam enim ibi sunt praestrigia
demonum, quaedam autem figmenta
poetica, quaedam similia uero, quaedam
non, quaedam ad delectationem stultorum.

Táin Bó Cúailnge

DZC

Sit down and come to order,
And I'll tell you what was done
Across the Irish border
At the risin of the sun.

First let me make confession
To all you dads and mums:
My dignified profession
Is makin lambeg drums.

I'm happy when I'm steamin
A shell of quartered oak,
Or when a 'scarf' I'm seamin,
Or when I've skins to soak.

There's people always tryin
To learn the trade for cheap,
And a lot of boys is dyin
To know what's in my steep.

For you can catch a nanny,
And skin her head to tail,
Yet if you aren't canny
With your steep, you're bound to fail.

You're tired of explanation,
But I want you all to note:
If the drum's your occupation,
You need supplies of goat.

In spring my bus'ness picks up,
And repairs get out of hand;
People give me drums to fix up
For every kind of band.

Last week my head was achin
When I added up my sums;
I had to find the makins
For twenty lambeg drums.

The skins I had amounted
To nothin more than six!
I saw, once I had counted,
That I was in a fix.

But then the phone starts ringin.
'Hello, who's there?' I quotes,
And a southern voice is singin,
'I know where there's forty goats.'

He says, 'I have two neighbours,
And they've stolen sheep from me;
If their goats will help your labours,
You can have them all for free.'

He gave me clear directions
Which I'll not share with you,
In case you have connections
With the helpful boys in blue.

Next Sunday saw me speedin
Like somebody inspired
Beside two friends map-readin
In the lorry that I'd hired.

The sun was risin barely
As we began our flight.
(I had to be home early
For a church parade that night.)

We didn't see a sinner;
For joy I could have sung.
I said, 'We're on a winner!'
My friend said, 'Houl your tongue.'

And then we took a turnin;
I checked my written notes,
And soon we were discernin
A meadow full of goats.

My friends went round and caught them,
And brought them up to me;
I personally shot them
Beneath an elder tree.

And one by one we bled them,
Those late lamented goats;
The meadow looked like bedlam
Once we had cut their throats.

At first the rest did nothin;
They showed no sign of fear.
By the time I'd shot a dozen,
They got the main idea.

I had to run in circles;
The work was gettin hard!
There was six or seven quare kills
At a range of thirty yards.

To madness I was driven
When I ran clean out of lead;
There was seven goats still livin
Would have been far safer dead.

My friend said it was his turn,
And around the field did leap
With a big mahogany Disprin,
And put seven goats to sleep.

We loaded up the lorry,
And fairly pushed the pace;
I was in a state of worry
Till we got back safe to base.

So listen, males and females,
If your lambeg needs repair,
You can give me all the details,
For I have some skins to spare.

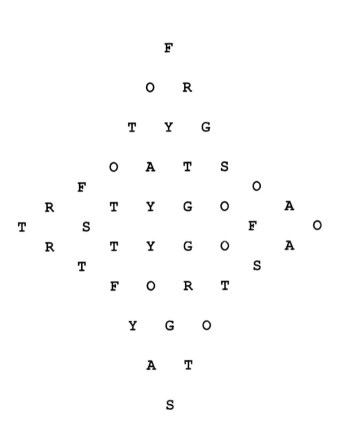

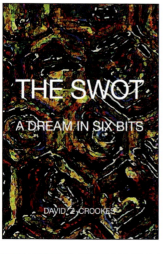
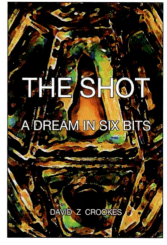

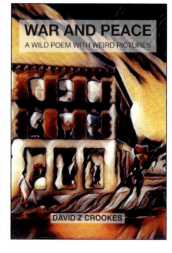

FORTY GOATS follows DZC's

previous four books.

His brilliant trilogy

THE SHOT, THE SWOT and

THE SLOT are all poems of 72 verses.

After that came the superb

WAR AND PEACE.

All four are available from

Shanway Press and also Amazon.